D1258143

SandCastle™

Baby Mammals

It's a Baby Gray Wolf!

Kelly Doudna

Consulting Editor, Diane Craig, M.A./Reading Specialist

ABDO
Publishing Company

Published by ABDO Publishing Company, 8000 West 78th Street, Edina, Minnesota 55439.

Editor: Pam Price
Content Developer: Nancy Tuminelly
Cover and Interior Design and Production: Mighty Media
Photo Credits: Corbis (D. Robert & Lorri Franz), Creatas, Peter Arnold Inc. (Steven Kazlowski, J.L. Klein & M.L. Hubert, H. Reinhard, Lynn Rogers, D. Usher, R. Wittek)

Library of Congress Cataloging-in-Publication Data

Doudna, Kelly, 1963-
  It's a baby gray wolf! / Kelly Doudna.
    p. cm. -- (Baby mammals)
  ISBN 978-1-60453-024-7
1. Wolves--Infancy--Juvenile literature. I. Title.

QL737.C22D68 2008
599.773'139--dc22

                    2007033747

SandCastle™ Level: Fluent

SandCastle™ books are created by a team of professional educators, reading specialists, and content developers around five essential components—phonemic awareness, phonics, vocabulary, text comprehension, and fluency—to assist young readers as they develop reading skills and strategies and increase their general knowledge. All books are written, reviewed, and leveled for guided reading, early reading intervention, and Accelerated Reader® programs for use in shared, guided, and independent reading and writing activities to support a balanced approach to literacy instruction. The SandCastle™ series has four levels that correspond to early literacy development. The levels are provided to help teachers and parents select appropriate books for young readers.

Emerging Readers
(no flags)

Beginning Readers
(1 flag)

Transitional Readers
(2 flags)

Fluent Readers
(3 flags)

SandCastle™ would like to hear from you. Please send us your comments and suggestions.
sandcastle@abdopublishing.com

Vital Statistics
for the Gray Wolf

BABY NAME
pup, cub

NUMBER IN LITTER
1 to 14, average 4 to 6

WEIGHT AT BIRTH
about 1 pound

AGE OF INDEPENDENCE
2 to 3 years

ADULT WEIGHT
40 to 170 pounds

LIFE EXPECTANCY
5 to 7 years

A mother wolf finds a cave, crevice, or hole to use as a den. There, she gives birth to her pups.

The pups begin to explore when they are two or three weeks old.

Wolves live in groups called packs. Pack members include the mother, father, and older siblings of the pups.

Pack members help care for the pups. This gives the mother a break.

When pups are two weeks old, they begin eating food that is regurgitated by adult pack members.

Wolves hunt as a group. They prey on large animals, such as deer and moose.

Wolves only catch about 1 out of every 10 animals they chase.

Wolves don't have any enemies in the wild. However, wolves will attack rival wolves in fights over territory.

Wolves are famous for howling. Wolves howl to warn other packs to stay away. A wolf also howls to attract the attention of its pack members.

Wolf pups are very playful. They learn important hunting skills by play fighting with each other.

Pups begin hunting with the pack when they are about six months old.

Young wolves stay with
their birth packs until they
are two or three years old.
Then they leave to form
new packs.

Fun Fact
About the Gray Wolf

Wolves began living closely with humans about 14,000 years ago. They gradually became the best friends we love today. All domestic dog breeds, from small to tall, are a subspecies of the gray wolf.

Glossary

crevice – a narrow space between two surfaces.

den – a small hollow used by an animal for shelter.

domestic – living with or near humans.

expectancy – an expected or likely amount.

gradually – happening very slowly over time.

independence – the state of no longer needing others to care for or support you.

prey – to hunt or catch an animal for food.

regurgitate – to bring food that has already been swallowed back into the mouth.

rival – competing for the same thing.

sibling – one's brother or sister.

territory – an area that is occupied and defended by an animal or a group of animals.

To see a complete list of SandCastle™ books and other nonfiction titles from ABDO Publishing Company, visit **www.abdopublishing.com**.

8000 West 78th Street, Edina, MN 55439

800-800-1312 • 952-831-1632 fax